DEPRESSION
RESET

RELIEF AND HELP FOR ADULTS, PARENTS OR TEENS
with a 10-step practical solution to cure depression naturally

SARAH KOUS

Depression: A Practical Approach
by Sarah Kous

Digital Editing by Alex Kous

Copyright © by Sarah Kous 2018
Revised Edition 2018

All rights reserved

No part of this book may be reproduced in any form or by any electronic or mechanical means, including information storage and retrieval systems, without written permission from the author, except for the use of brief quotations in the book review.

DEPRESSION: A PRACTICAL APPROACH

Don't fight it. Don't ignore it. There is hope!

RESET YOUR BRAIN IN TWO WEEKS

This no-nonsense, no-fluff, no pop-psychology, no quackery, no BS program is for anyone who struggles with depression. It is based on the advice and guidance I have given to patients, friends and family with this condition, derived from 40 years experience as a mental health nurse, and now supported by neuroscience.

Genuine depression is a mood disorder that has no direct psychological cause and, while the suggestions in this book will help anyone — yes *anyone* — it should not to be confused with grieving or a crisis situation.

Depression is characterized by the presence of five or more of these symptoms over two weeks or longer:

1. Depressed mood or irritable most of the day, nearly every day.
2. Decreased interest or pleasure in most activities, most of each day.
3. Significant weight change (5%) or change in appetite.
4. Change in sleep: Insomnia or hypersomnia.
5. Change in activity.
6. Fatigue or loss of energy.
7. Guilt/worthlessness: Feelings of worthlessness or excessive or inappropriate guilt.
8. Concentration: diminished ability to think or concentrate, or more indecisiveness.
9. Suicidality: Thoughts of death or suicide, or has suicide plan.[1]

This book also assumes that the reader has had a full medical check-up for health conditions that can be masked by what appears to be depression, such as thyroid disorders, vitamin and mineral deficiencies or medication side-effects, and that the mood disorder is the primary condition. It is also essential that you are checked for a condition known as Sleep Apnea (discussed in Appendix 1).

Please consult your doctor before using the methods outlined in this book. Don't stop taking any regular medication without your doctor's permission. If you are suicidal, this book is not for you at this stage: please see a doctor immediately.

Just The Facts

The interventions outlined here are practical, rather than philosophical or psychological, and the focus will be on *what you can do now*. Because lifestyle changes need to be implemented immediately, I have kept this book as short and light as possible. You are going to reset your brain, and the last thing you need right now is to be burdened with a verbose and lengthy tome.

Each intervention has two parts: **The Science Behind It** and the **Practical Application**. Since we all love our phones and devices, and advances in technology make self management even easier, Apps, downloads or gadget suggestions will be highlighted with this icon 🖥 The suggestions in this book need to be patiently followed for at least two weeks before changes will become noticeable.

TABLE OF CONTENTS

The Revolving Door Syndrome ... 1
The Rotating Body-Clock ... 7
Reset 1: Start Here ... 15
Reset 2: Feed Your Mind ... 19
Reset 3: Get Your Daily Lux Quota ... 27
Reset 4: Beyond Blue: How Kelvin Can Help ... 35
Reset 5: From E-motion to Motion ... 43
Reset 6: Speed Up And Slow Down (At The Right Times) ... 53
Reset 7: Sleep Spot-On ... 59
Reset 8: Tweak Your Core Body Temperature ... 69
Reset 9: Fine-Tune Your Environment To Lower Anxiety ... 75
Reset 10: Halt The Rumination ... 79
Reset 11: Avoid The Self Medicating Trap ... 85
12: Reset For Teenagers ... 89
13 Regenerate: Create Your Personalized Plan ... 97
14 Revise: Your Daily Mood Log ... 101
15: Remission Mastery ... 105
Appendix 1: Sleep Apnea ... 109
Appendix 2: Night Shift ... 111
Appendix 3: Jet Lag ... 113

THE REVOLVING DOOR SYNDROME

Mental health nurses, unlike doctors, psychologists and other health professions, are in a unique position in being able to observe patients over 24-hour periods, and for six to ten hours at a time. Although we dispense medication, write reports, counsel, act as mediators, fetch clean towels, and generally multi-task, the underlying essential of our job is that of *observation*. We are trained to observe for changes in mood, health, cognition, behavior, speech, and thought content. We monitor for levels of self-care or neglect, danger signals, and adverse reactions to medications, and we are in this observation mode from the time we clock-on until we clock-off.

Over the past 40 years, thousands of patients have passed through the mental health units I have worked on. They have come from every social stratum, age group, profession and lifestyle: and all have unique backgrounds to their problems. But there is one thing almost every new admission has in common. No matter what the psychiatric diagnosis, they all report disturbed and restless nights, unusual sleep patterns or severe insomnia. I even remember one patient who claimed they hadn't slept for an entire fortnight!

During the day at the inpatient unit, I would frequently find my patients napping in their rooms. Their curtains would be drawn and the room darkened. They regularly missed meals. On afternoon and night shift, the same patients were often observed eating at odd times: even drinking strong coffee in the middle of the night. Unable to sleep, yet bored and distressed, and wanting escape from their problems, they would pass their night hours watching TV, or playing on their phones or laptops.

When I discussed these daily habits with them, and suggested they make some changes, many simply dismissed my advice, while others expressed their frustration at being incapable of change. It was as though their bad habits, together with their mental state, were in a vicious circle they couldn't escape. But once these same patients were stabilized with the regular routine of the inpatient unit, and medication adjusted where necessary, their sleep patterns returned to normal and their illness went into remission.

The correlation between sleep and mental illness is well known among experienced mental health professionals, but the link between cause and effect is still hazy. Was the disturbed sleep *a result of* the mental illness, or did lack of sleep *trigger* the disorder? Officially, the jury is still out. But in most cases, the patient's recent history included stressful external events that caused restless nights. There were others with a recent history of drug or alcohol abuse, the birth of a baby, a long plane trip across time zones, or even excessive Coca Cola or coffee consumption. In fact, the *Diagnostic and Statistical Manual of Mental Disorders V* includes 'Caffeine Induced' disorders in its extensive catalogue. If disturbed sleep was secondary to the illness, why was there nearly always a pre-admission history of well-known factors that typically disrupt the 24-hour sleep pattern? And why could most people survive lack of sleep without serious consequences?

The average stay in a mental health inpatient unit is two weeks, which coincides with the average time it takes for the body-clock to fully readjust. Two weeks is also the 'magic' time it takes for anti-depressants to begin working. Between admission and discharge, the changes in the patient's mood and functioning are often dramatic. Relaxed and smiling, these patients would be discharged from hospital and the future looked bright. Unfortunately, most would return home to the same destructive lifestyle habits, and their problems continued. Marriages split up. Jobs were lost. People ended up on welfare. The inclination for mood disorders to relapse, resulting in a return to the inpatient unit every few months prompted mental health professionals to coin the well-known, but rather cynical phrase, "Revolving Door Syndrome," reflecting frustration and helplessness at the continual re-admissions of some patients. But it doesn't have to be this way! And mental health nurses with many years experience have been privy to at least part of the solution.

The thesis of this book, then, is that **firstly**, the sleep-wake cycle is crucial to well-being for people predisposed to depression, and our biological clocks can be programmed with practical interventions that will benefit anyone. **Secondly**, sleep is not an isolated phenomenon: it is connected to the way we live during our waking hours, and some people, at certain stages in their lives, are more sensitive to environmental changes than others.

Our goal is euthymia (say it: *you-thymia*), which is Greek for 'good spirits,' and is mental-health-speak for a stable, non-depressed mental state or mood. Unlike *happiness*, which tends to change with life's ups and downs, euthymia is not an emotion. You can be both euthymic *and* sad: the difference being that you are in control of your thoughts, mood and actions. When you are euthymic, you get your life back, your sleep improves, the daily routine doesn't seem like a chore anymore, you quit wondering when you're going to feel better, and you suddenly find yourself being creative and productive again.

In the following chapters you will be shown how to reset your brain so that the only thing that 'revolves' is your 24hr body clock: not your mood ... or the hospital door.

THE ROTATING BODY-CLOCK

Close The Revolving Door For Good

THE SCIENCE BEHIND IT

Nothing happens in isolation. When a gun fires, there is recoil. When a bird flies up, its wings push down. When a fish swims forwards, its fins push backwards. Analogous to Newton's Third Law of Motion, *"For every action, there is an equal and opposite reaction,"* our brain chemistry works on a similar action-reaction basis, where imbalances in one zone will cause imbalances in another.

Brain Chemistry

In short, neurotransmitters and hormones carry messages and exchange information within your nervous system, directing your body's organs and systems to speed up or slow down. They also regulate body temperature, blood pressure, levels of digestive enzymes and various hormones, with innumerable fluctuations throughout the day. There are just two brain chemicals you need to know about for now: ***melatonin and serotonin***. Melatonin is a hormone that is produced by the Pineal Gland behind the eyes, and it regulates sleep and wakefulness. Serotonin is a neurotransmitter.

Melatonin, also known as the Hormone of Darkness, makes you feel sleepy. It slows you down. It lowers your mood. Melatonin *must* lower it at night because you won't sleep if your mood is too elevated. So melatonin is a natural and healthy *depressant.* It is also an anti-oxidant that helps to heal your body while you sleep.

Serotonin, on the other hand, wakes you up, lifts your mood and energizes you so that you can tackle daily activities.

Many anti-depressants operate by increasing serotonin levels. These medications don't suit everyone, and sometimes — especially with teens and the elderly — they can even have paradoxical effects, where the depression or anxiety worsens. Anti-depressants are also notorious for causing weight gain and, apart from making you feel even worse, obesity can cause sleep apnea (see Appendix 3) which can cause insomnia, which worsens depression. However, this book is not suggesting you stop taking anti-depressants or other psychotropic medications but offering a program that can work in conjunction with, or without, medications, depending on your doctor's advice.

There are natural ways to increase serotonin levels, and you don't need to buy expensive vitamins or herbs or go on special diets. 'Natural,' in our context, means naturally tweaking the 24-hour cycle of sleeping and waking, that we call *The Circadian Rhythm.*

Circadian contains the word: circle. Imagine the top half of the circle is the day, and the bottom half: the night. This next point is crucial: *what we do in the day has a major impact on our sleep patterns at night.* Although neuro-biology is a very complex subject, all you need to know for this program is that melatonin and serotonin work in synchrony like a see-saw, and our bodies should run on a 24-hour clock. Our Autonomic Nervous System (ANS) is the control system in our brain and spinal cord that regulates bodily functions like heart rate, digestion, breathing and circulation, without our thinking or awareness. The interesting thing is that our internal clock *memorizes and repeats the ANS's actions from the previous 24–72 hours*, also without our conscious control.

In this picture, observe the contrasts on opposite sides of the circle, and note how the night and day synchronistically serve each other. How does your current routine compare?

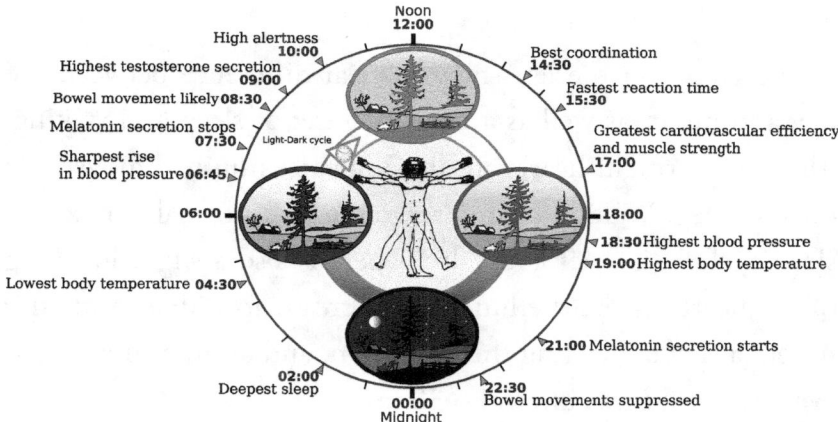

And here are two graphs that show pulse rates over a 24-hour period, comparing the data of people without mental illness, and those with depression. Because heart rates reflect the activities of the ANS, they also offer a picture of the person's circadian cycle over the 24hrs.

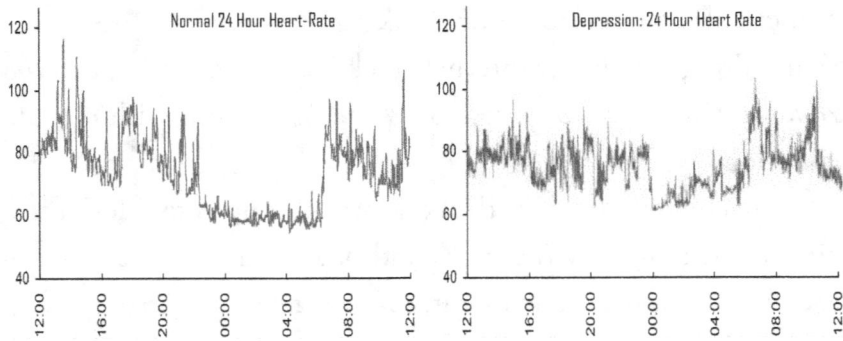

The graph on the left shows a clear difference between the day and night, as well as a distinct onset of sleep and waking. The low overnight heart rate also indicates minimal movement during sleep. Waking during the night — a normal part of the sleep cycle — is brief and calm. There is also a slight lowering of the heart rate before lunch, an increase at midday and after lunch, a slowing during the afternoon, and another increase at evening meal time, around 6.30pm.

The graph on the right, however, shows minimal difference between the night and day heart rates.[2] It is as if the body and brain do not know what time it is, and whether to relax or speed up. Also note the increase in heart-rate as the night progresses: this is a typical sloping pattern for depression. Anxiety disorders show a similar disturbed pattern, though with a reverse slope at night.

Our natural circadian rhythms are altered, for better or worse, with:
- Food
- Seasons
- Illness

- Physical activity
- Drugs and alcohol
- Nicotine
- House lighting
- Pain
- Medications
- Temperature
- Noise vs quiet
- Light and Dark
- Caffeine products
- Sleep Apnea
- Menopause
- Some medications
- Lack of, or too much, stimulation
- Psychological issues, like stress, grieving or anxiety
- Jet Lag: See Appendix 1 for ways to reduce Jet Lag if you are prone to depression.
- Night Shift: See Appendix 2
- A New Baby: Post Partum Depression is the official name for a depressive episode following the birth of a baby. This particular problem is beyond the scope of this book, but it is interesting to note that this is another instance where the sleep-wake cycle affects the mood and mental state of sensitive people.

You *can* overcome depression, and the solutions that have been proven to work will be outlined in the following chapters.

RESET ONE: START HERE

Record your baseline data.

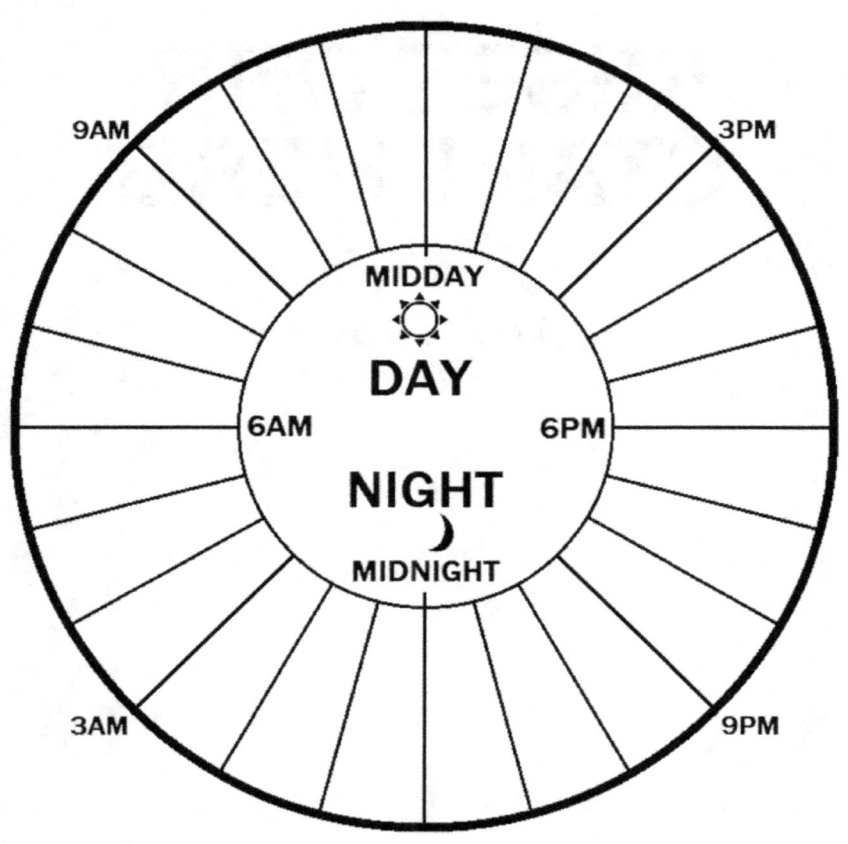

PRACTICAL APPLICATION

- Print this circle with your printer.
- Lightly shade in the hours you *currently sleep* and leave your waking hours unshaded.
- Google *sunset and sunrise times*, and pencil in this data.
- Shade in the *current hours of darkness* for where you live.
- Record the times you eat *meals, snacks*, and drink *tea, coffee, fizzy drinks, juices* or *alcohol*.
- Use another color to shade in the hours you are facing a *laptop, computer or TV screen*.
- Note down your *work hours*, and if you exercise, note that as well.
- Pencil in your *mood rating* for each hour over the past day or two: -2: very low, -1: low, 0: neutral, +1 euthymic, +2 euthymic and productive, +3 euthymic and fully functioning.
- Are there any patterns?
- Print out a second Circadian Circle to create your new lifestyle as you read each chapter.

In the next few chapters, we will address these issues one by one, beginning with the easier steps. Once these externals have been dealt with, we will look at solutions to rumination and other mood disorder problems, followed by a plan to manage remission.

RESET 2: FEED YOUR MIND

*Program your internal clock with
a consistent meal schedule.*

THE SCIENCE BEHIND IT

Pavlov's Dog

Ivan Pavlov's famous experiment in Classical Conditioning involved a hand bell, a bowl of food, and a pet dog. Pavlov would ring the bell whenever his dog ate food. After a period of repetition, he tried ringing the bell without the food, and his dog automatically salivated. The dog's involuntary Autonomic Nervous System (ANS) had learnt to associate the bell with the food. Even though the dog could not see or smell food, his brain had been conditioned to *expect* it.

Here is another politically incorrect story to do with food, repetition and our ANS.

Baby Advice From The Pub

"Our 10-month-old daughter used to wake up at exactly 2am and scream for a bottle of milk," an elderly Scotsman recounted to me once. *"My wife was tired of this, so I offered to take the night feed. A week later, I was chatting with a friend in the pub, telling him how shattered I was, and he advised me to give the little lass a bottle of warm water for her 2am feed instead of milk. At first, I laughed. She'd scream more. 'No,' he said, 'it really works.' So, I tried the warm water that very night. It worked: she went to sleep and didn't wake up at night again, and started eating more during the day."*

While this book is not advising anyone try either of these scenarios, Pavlov's dog and Baby Advice From The Pub are true stories that demonstrate how highly adaptable and programable our bodies are.

Two important points here:
1. All food is a serotonin enhancer.
2. The timings of your meals cue your biological clock to know what time of day it is.

The Food Clock

All food is broken down into sugars, fats and proteins, depending on what your body needs at the time. High sugar foods will give you a quicker "hit" than food that releases sugar more slowly, ie bread, pasta, meat, vegetables, milk products and nuts etc. Caffeine, found in coffee, chocolate, tea and many soft drinks, is a well-known serotonin booster, and there is no harm in indulging in caffeine or sugar products, provided you are eating a balanced diet, and avoiding caffeine products from six hours before bedtime.

Sugar and caffeine are also common cravings during the evening when there is a natural — and needed — slump in serotonin. When this happens, food and caffeine will perk us up again, but consumption in the evening will delay the onset of melatonin, and we won't fall asleep as easily. If we eat at night, we signal to our brains that it is day, and our serotonin levels will increase, while melatonin will cease. Our puzzled ANS thought it was night, and now it is receiving messages suggesting it is day, so it tumbles into a confused overdrive, and exhaustion and mood disorders are the result.

Important: *Your digestive system needs to fast 12–13 hours overnight to communicate to your brain that it is time to sleep.*

Post Lunch Slump

Circadian Cycle experts say that many of us are 'biphasic,' meaning that twice a day our core body temperature drops and melatonin kicks in. The big one, as we have seen, is at night. But there is a mini phase in the early afternoon. For many of us, but on a much smaller scale than at night, our core temperature drops at this time, and we experience a post-lunch slump. If you must nap in the day, limit it to no more than 30 minutes in a light room, and not in your bedroom. A lighter lunch followed by a brisk walk outdoors will change your biological clock's napping habit.

Food cravings

Some cravings do indeed shed light on what's missing from our diet. During your eating hours, be sensitive to your body's needs, and if you crave a certain food, try eating a little. Provided your diet is balanced, and you not eating in the evening or night, enjoy some chocolate. In fact, it may even be beneficial for health.[3] Once you have reprogrammed your ANS, using the advice in this book, and are following a balanced diet, cravings will either disappear, or at least be dramatically reduced.

Warm Milk Before Bed?

There are some data suggesting that a glass of warm milk before bed helps induce sleep, and milk does indeed contain some soporific substances, but it also contains calories which mean energy, digestion, higher core body temperature, and possible sleep disruption in sensitive people. The bottom line? Try both ways and discover what works for you: strict fasting for 12–13 hours ... *or* fasting 12–13 hours *except for* a small glass of warm milk an hour before bedtime.

PRACTICAL APPLICATION

You can re-program your biological clock so that your ANS will know what time of day or night it is, speed up or slow down accordingly, and produce serotonin and melatonin at the right times. It will take at least two weeks to fully reset your biological clock.

- Fasting for 12–13 hours overnight is essential, not just for your brain chemistry and sleep quality, but overall health. All meals and snacks should be consumed inside an 11–12 hour window during the day, for example a 7am–6pm window.
- Avoid heavy or high fat meals in the evening.
- Fasting should begin at least two hours before bedtime. Fasting means that only water should be taken by mouth for a 12–13 hour period overnight.
- If you feel hungry in the evening, even though you have eaten dinner, resist the urge to eat. It is not hunger you are feeling, but a change in brain chemistry from serotonin to melatonin. The hunger will subside if you do not feed it!
- If you are in the habit of eating or drinking at night, you may wake up hungry. *Resist the temptation ... or drink a glass of water.* The change might not be immediate, as it was with the baby, but *it will pass*.
- Eat breakfast within an hour or less of waking, but at least 12 hours after your evening meal. So, if you finished eating

by 7pm the previous night, breakfast should be no earlier than 7–8am the following day.
- Eat your meals at the same set times each day. Note the time you have breakfast. Count forward 10–11 hours. This is the time you should eat your evening meal. For example: if you ate breakfast at 7am, all eating must be finished by 7pm, or before if possible. So begin eating dinner at 5.30pm or 6pm. Lunch can be eaten at any time between those two meal times, but choose a time and stick to it.
- Eat a healthy and balanced diet. Recent data suggests that the very tasty, balanced and easy to follow *Mediterranean Diet* might be helpful with depression with some people.[4]
- Fill in the Circadian Circle (page 16) with your new meal times that best fit with your daily commitments.

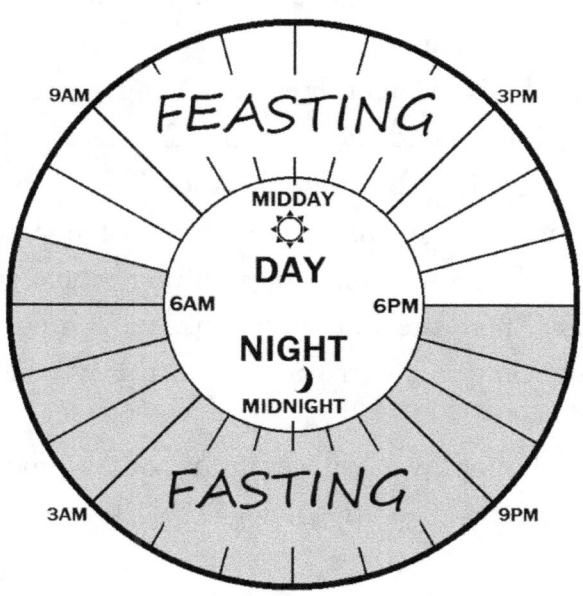

📟 APPS

- https://www.mynetdiary.com although this app is designed for weight loss, it can also tell you how many calories you need each day to maintain your healthy weight, and keep track of your meals, so you won't feel hungry at night.
- https://www.myfitnesspal.com can also track your calories and other fitness goals.

There are also plenty of Mediterranean Diet apps with recipe suggestions.

SET YOUR BODY CLOCK BY YOUR DIET

Our sleep clocks have a really aggravating way of demanding obedience. But the good news is that our ANS is programmable, and our eating patterns can set the 24-hour circadian cycle where we need it to be. If we establish a routine, our biological clock will follow suit.

The title of this chapter is Feed Your Mind, because your food intake and timings 'feed' messages to your brain about what time of day or night it is. But the expression 'feed your mind' can also be a metaphor for what you take in via the senses: reading inspiring books, conversing with uplifting people, listening to inspirational podcasts and audiobooks, attending a religious service, or going to an art gallery, and this will be expanded upon in Reset 6.

Firstly, though, we will examine other environmental influences on mood and the biological clock.

RESET 3: GET YOUR DAILY LUX QUOTA

Program your internal clock with light and dark.

THE SCIENCE BEHIND IT

For millennia, we humans lived in synchrony with the sun and, until the advent of artificial lighting, it was our main source of illumination. Candles and open fires offered a meagre glow after sunset and were expensive, so most people simply retired to bed early. But today, our evenings are typically radiating with bright lights, TVs, laptops and iPhones, and we take these gadgets pretty much for granted. But light at the wrong time throws the body's biological clock out of whack. Sleep suffers. Worse, research shows that night light not only impacts mood disorders, but may also contribute to a range of other health problems from cancer to heart disease.

In centuries gone by, we spent most of our day working outdoors, but in our modern industrialized world, we spend 90% of our time indoors.[5] On top of that, our cities and towns are never dark. Because of Light Pollution, astronomers must haul their telescopes hundreds of miles from civilization if they want to see the night sky clearly. This Light Pollution map www.lightpollutionmap.info reveals how 'light' our world is at night. While Hong Kong is thought to be the most light-polluted city in the world, most cities expose urban dwellers to night-time light levels three to six times brighter than people in small towns.

So, in short, we often don't get enough light in the day, while at night we can't get away from it! Yet the effects of light have a powerful non-visual drug-like effect on our body and mind, similar to drinking a double expresso. Further, sleep improves following more exposure to daylight during the day, especially in the morning.[6]

*The important thing to remember is that your biological clock is directed by the **timing**, **intensity**, and **consistency** of light exposure.*

This chart shows how sources of light differ. A lux is a measure of brightness of light, and reveals how much the outdoors differs to the indoors.

LIGHT SOURCE	LUX
Direct Sunlight	108,000
Full Daylight	10,000
Overcast Day	1000
Very Dark Day	107
Standard Office	300-500
Average Living Room	50-100
Average Computer Screen	50
iPhone	20
1 Candle at 1' distance	10
Full Moon	0.25
Overcast Night	0.0001

Summers in northern Europe, Alaska and Canada experience only a few hours of darkness at night, while the winters are long and dark, and Seasonal Affective Disorder (SAD) is a well-known condition there. The lack of light throughout those long dark months affects serotonin production and, as it should now be clear, those with sensitive circadian rhythms experience a depressed mood.

Light therapy is an effective treatment for SAD, and it involves sitting close to a special light source that is far more intense than normal indoor lighting. The light treatment begins early in the morning and, while some people only need to use it once or twice, most require at least a few days, some need several weeks. You can buy boxes that emit therapeutic light intensity (10,000 lux) with a minimal amount of UV light without a prescription, but it is best to work with a professional who can monitor your response.

Since there are direct connections between the retina and the Pineal Gland, it is important that light, or darkness, enters through the eyes, even if they are closed. Melatonin secretion is controlled by the circadian clock, and is suppressed by bright light.

This cross-section diagram of the head shows the position of the Pineal Gland, which is sometimes known as the 'Third Eye,' and how light, or darkness, communicates the time of day via the eyes.

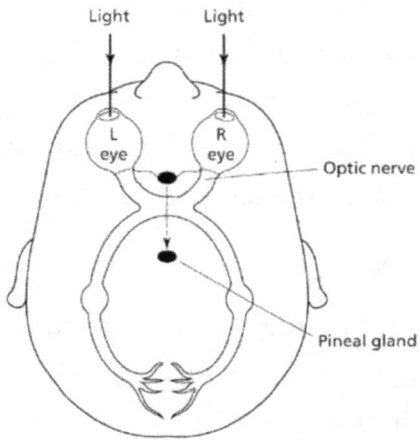

When the Pineal Gland senses the dark of night, it begins to produce melatonin and reduce its serotonin counterpart, *provided that* you don't consume any food or drink, except water.

PRACTICAL APPLICATION

Twelve Hours of Light

- Maximize your exposure to daylight during the day, especially during the morning, and particularly between 7–9am for best effects. Consistency is essential.
- Move your work desk next as close to a window as you can.
- If you live in an area with 10–12 hours of darkness, wake up as the sun rises. Catching a few extra hours of natural daylight can help your brain chemistry levels adjust more naturally. We often forget that we wake up a few hours after sunrise and miss two hours of lux quota.
- Consider buying a light box (eBay sells them) if there are fewer than 10 hours of light per day during winter, or if you are unable to leave the house. Read a book or work on your laptop while you sit next to your light box.
- Avoid napping during the day: eat a light lunch only, and get moving in the afternoon.
- Optimize your home and workspace for natural lighting. It means a bright, almost daylight-like indoor space.

Twelve Hours of Darkness

- Even dim light can interfere with the circadian rhythm and melatonin production. A mere eight lux—a small table lamp—can have an effect in sensitive people.[7]

- Avoid looking at screens, phones, kindles and e-readers beginning 2–3 hours before bed.
- If you wake before 6am, stay in the darkened room in bed until that time. If disturbing thoughts and feelings are overwhelming, distract yourself with something you can do in relative darkness, ie play a game on your phone with the screen-light maximally dimmed and blue-light blocked (more on that in Chapter 4).
- You might want to investigate Smart Lighting which can be programmed to dim and change color, simulate sunset and sunrise. Brand names include Philips Hue and TorchStar.
- Fill in the Circadian Circle (page 16) with your new light and dark hours that best fit with your daily commitments.

In the next chapter, we will examine a further dimension in lighting on mood and health: *its Kelvin*.

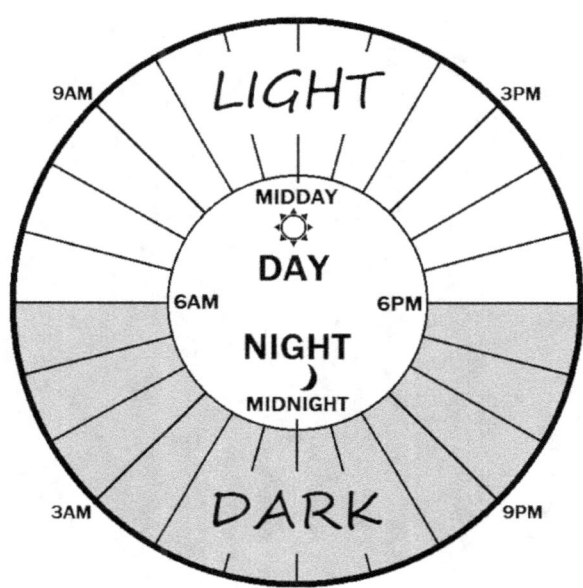

RESET 4: BEYOND BLUE: HOW KELVIN CAN HELP

Program your biological clock with the right color at the right time.

THE SCIENCE BEHIND IT

While the intensity and timing of light exposure affects our biological clocks, there is a further dimension to light: its color. Not to be confused with the pseudoscience *Color Therapy*, or *Chromotherapy*, the colors emitted by light sources do in fact affect brain chemistry.

The Impact of Warm and Cool Colors

For thousands of years, our hunter-gather ancestors slept outside and were gently woken by the warm hues of sunrise gradually changing from red to orange, yellow to blue-white, and increasing in lux. It turns out that we have a fascinating mechanism that communicates information to our biological clock via *color*.

Melanopsin is a photoreceptor at the back of our eyes that is especially primed to pick up color frequencies that signal daylight and time to wake up, even with our eyes closed. After absorbing these color frequencies, melanopsin communicates directly to the Autonomic Nervous System. Peaking at 480nm, or 6000 Kelvin, which is a similar spectrum to the midday sun, this receptor stimulates connections between areas of the brain that process emotion and language, lifting mood and problem-solving ability.

Without getting into complicated physics, colors emit different wavelengths that stimulate our retinal receptors at faster or slower frequencies. Of visible light, blue has the fastest frequencies, while red: the slowest. Exposure to blue-enriched white light during daylight hours, especially in the morning, results in sounder sleep at night. But this frequency is also most disruptive at night, and the slightest exposure, even with our eyes closed, can interrupt the production of melatonin because our brain still thinks it is day.

Apart from the sun, other sources of blue-white light include digital screens, TVs, computers, laptops, smart phones and tablets, electronic devices, and full spectrum lighting. Most lightbulbs sold today show the Kelvin measurement, and 5000–6500K is considered a good match to sunlight, and therefore suitable for indoor day lighting.

(Caution: indirect light is advised: too much direct blue-light can cause eye damage.[9])

Kelvin is a measurement of color temperature: from warm reds to cool blues. This chart shows the Kelvin of various light sources.

Kelvin	Source
1700K	Match flame, low pressure sodium lamps
1850K	Candle flame, sunset/sunrise
2400K	Standard incandescent lamps
2550K	Soft white incandescent lamps
2700K	Soft white compact fluorescent and LED lamps
3000K	Warm white compact fluorescent and LED lamps
3200K	Studio lamps, photofloods, etc.
5000K	Early morning or late afternoon daylight / Fluorescent lamps
500–6000K	Noon daylight, electronic flash
6500K	Daylight, overcast
6500–9500K	LCD or CRT screen

As you can see in the picture below, blue has the fastest wavelengths, while red: the slowest. Exposure to dimmed red lighting in the evening is far less disruptive on sleep patterns and even makes us feel sleepy.

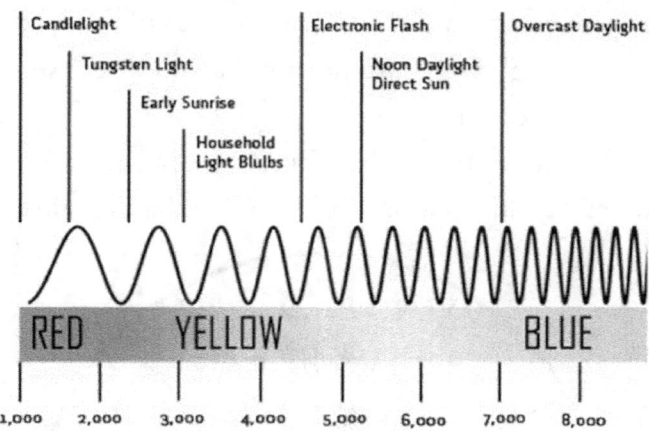

PRACTICAL APPLICATION

- If you live in an area of the world where the sun doesn't rise much over the horizon, enhance your day areas with lighting. Lightbulbs measuring 5000–6500K can be bought at most hardware stores. Avoid looking directly at these lights.
- If, on the other hand, you live in an area of the world where the UV is high after midmorning, avoid direct sunlight on bare skin after this time.
- Stay as far away from white-blue light in the evening.
- Add helpful information to your Circadian Circle (page 16).

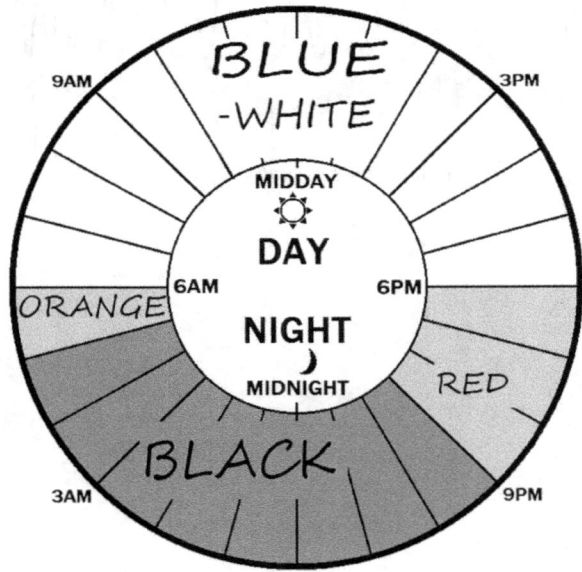

 If you use a computer or laptop, *f.lux*: https://justgetflux.com is a fabulous tool. This free and easy two-minute download can be programmed to your time zone, so that during the day you receive the ideal 6000 Kelvin, automatically switching to a warm dimmer screen in 'Winding Down Mode' at 2500K after

6pm, and slowly dropping to 1900K half an hour before bed. There is a sunrise at 2500K for half an hour the next morning, after which it switches to a bright blue-white screen again. One of the great things about this app is that the color change in the evening also acts as a gentle reminder that it is wind-down time. It will also remind you when you have nine hours left until your wake-up time, which is the best time to shut down the devices.

Evening and Night

- Consider wearing blue-blocking glasses (bought on eBay) if you use screens in the evening.
- Change your bedside lamp bulb to a red one, and use lamps with red or orange bulbs in the living areas during evening, especially two hours before your regular bedtime.
- 🖥 iPhones and Apple Mac devices can be switched to 'warm' and 'dim' as follows:
    » Go to Settings.
    » Tap on Display and Brightness.
    » Adjust the brightness on the next screen.
    » Choose "Nightshift" and set your phone to automatically switch to a 'warm' dimmer screen, meaning less blue light.
    » Windows computers also have a color control setting (menu > color).
- 🖥 Optional gadget: you can buy alarm clocks on eBay that simulate a sunrise, so that you can transition from darkness to red, orange, yellow then blue, instead of the abrupt change from darkness to bright blue light first thing in the morning: just like our hunter-gatherer ancestors experienced.

Along with the changes in your eating habits and lighting, your activity levels also program your brain chemistry. The best and latest information on this will be the subject of the next two chapters.

RESET 5: FROM E-MOTION TO MOTION

"I regret that workout"—said no one ever

THE SCIENCE
(AND A LITTLE PHILOSOPHY)
BEHIND IT

Probably the *last* thing you feel like doing with a low mood is bopping around a gym to zesty aerobics music. Just getting out of bed and into the light outside might feel like conquering Mount Everest. But exercise is not only essential for normal health, it is a tremendous serotonin booster. Furthermore, the anti-depressant effects are cumulative, meaning that the more you exercise the better you feel and for longer periods, even when you're not exercising.

Although the exact anti-depressant mechanism with exercise is not yet fully understood, it is thought to be a combination between these factors:

1. An increase in core body temperature during the day, which improves mood as well as sleep at night, since heart rate increases body heat.
2. An increase in brain chemicals that produce a feeling of well-being and calm.
3. Distraction from rumination and negative thoughts.
4. A feeling of self control and efficiency.
5. Improvement in sleep patterns.
6. Socializing, if done in a group.

But depression deludes us into thinking that we'll get out when we feel better. Unfortunately, what we don't see, is that *we do not feel better until we get out.*

Just Do It?

A unique feature of being human is free-will. Humans can act against their instincts, feelings and impulses: by contrast, animals cannot. Furthermore, we humans were not meant to be motionless, and it is therefore unnatural to be sitting or lying down all day, and we suffer health problems because of this modern sedentary lifestyle. The only way to change this is to engage our uniquely human trait of doing stuff in spite of our thoughts, in the face of our feelings and regardless of our instincts. Breathe. Keep going. It may not seem like it but, with these small steps, you will get better.

Exercise? Don't think about it: just do it!

However, if even simple exercise is an impossible hurdle at this stage, see your doctor. You may need a kick-start course of anti-depressants.

Which Exercise?

A recent study tested the effects of aerobic versus anaerobic activity on depression, and both groups experienced a significant reduction in depression scores. This is great news, because it means you can choose any exercise program you like.[10] However it is best to choose one that combines aerobic exercise in order to increase your core temperature.

Exercise Choices

- Aerobic: any vigorous continuous movement that increases heart rate, ie brisk walking, swimming, running or dancing.
- Strength Training: includes resistance training, plyometrics, weight lifting and sprinting.
- Calisthenics: involves body movements done at a medium aerobic pace without gym equipment. Examples include lunges, sit-ups, push-ups and pull-ups.
- Interval training: repetitions of short bursts of high-intensity exercise followed by low-intensity exercises or rest periods.
- Boot camps: these are timed, high-intensity circuits that combine aerobic and resistance exercises.
- Balance or stability programs include Pilates, Tai Chi and core-strength exercises.
- Flexibility programs: yoga or stretching.

Non-contact Martial Arts, like karate or taekwondo, training includes all the above, is sociable, fun, and it provides incentives like levels and belt gradings.

PRACTICAL IMPLEMENTATION

- Check with your doctor before embarking on an exercise program.
- Prioritize exercise, no matter how bad you feel: *just do it*.
- Avoid thinking about exercise: write down your goals and plan in the evening so you don't have to think it over the next day.
- Set Realistic Goals. For example, Day 1: walk 500m, Day 2: walk 750m, and so on. Goals keep you motivated and increase your chances of success.
- Exercise should be part of a daily routine, even if it's only 10 minutes to begin with. Another key component of exercise success is to stick to the same routine and timeslot.[11]
- Never miss a day, no matter how you feel or what the weather is. Adherence is increased by showing up each day.
- Choose an exercise regime that you can most easily adhere to. Walking might be easiest to begin with.
- Exercise outdoors where possible: get your sunlight exposure at the same time.
- If you can't walk or run around your neighborhood, consider joining a gym, or hiring or buying gym equipment for your home. Walking machines are best because they can be set with a timer and at a pace that you have to keep to, without thinking about it.
- 🖥 If you can only exercise indoors, Youtube has plenty of free exercise programs available.
- Keep an exercise log.

- 📱 Phones usually have a free inbuilt pedometer, which is useful for tracking your movement during the day. The recommended number of daily steps a healthy person should reach is 10,000, which is equivalent to about one and half hours of walking.
- 📱 Reduce the tedium of exercise with an ipod, audiobook, or workout with a friend or a group.
- Apart from your exercise routine, keep active throughout the day to maintain serotonin levels and program your body-clock.
- Avoid exercise three hours before bedtime: that's the time you want to lower your core body temperature.
- Add the word "exercise" to your Circadian Circle (page 16) at a time that best fits with your daily commitments, but preferably in the morning.

Exercise Goals and Plan

Set realistic goals for the coming week, below. Reward yourself with something after achieving each step. Rewards can include a massage, new workout clothes, a sports game, theatre or concert tickets, lunch at your favorite café, a new gadget, a pedicure, or new book, and so on.

Sample Exercise Plan
Fill in your goals below

Week 1	Exercise Goal: to walk 2km in 7 days	
Monday	Walk 500m	✓
Tuesday	Walk 750m	✓
Wednesday	Walk 1km	✓
Thursday	Walk 1.25km	✓
Friday	Walk 1.5km	✓
Saturday	Walk 1.75km	✓
Sunday	Walk 2km	✓
REWARD	Massage	✓
Week:	Exercise Goal:	
Monday		
Tuesday		
Wednesday		
Thursday		
Friday		
Saturday		
Sunday		
REWARD		
Week:	Exercise Goal:	
Monday		
Tuesday		
Wednesday		
Thursday		
Friday		
Saturday		
Sunday		
REWARD		

Printable Exercise Plan

Week:	Exercise Goal:	
Monday		
Tuesday		
Wednesday		
Thursday		
Friday		
Saturday		
Sunday		
REWARD		
Week:	Exercise Goal:	
Monday		
Tuesday		
Wednesday		
Thursday		
Friday		
Saturday		
Sunday		
REWARD		
Week:	Exercise Goal:	
Monday		
Tuesday		
Wednesday		
Thursday		
Friday		
Saturday		
Sunday		
REWARD		
Week:	Exercise Goal:	
Monday		
Tuesday		
Wednesday		
Thursday		
Friday		
Saturday		
Sunday		
REWARD		

RESET 6: SPEED UP AND SLOW DOWN (at the right times)

Keep your internal clock set by your activity level.

THE SCIENCE BEHIND IT

A common cause of depression in dogs is a lack of physical, mental, sensory or social stimulation. Dogs need walks, pats, curious toys to chew, interesting bones to gnaw on, challenging ball throws to run after, a variety of people and novel spaces to sniff out. Humans are no different in this way. During the day, our brains and bodies are constituted to receive multi-sensory stimulation in the forms of physical activity, intellectual challenges, sensory information and social interactions.

While people differ in their need for stimulation quota, keeping active during the day not only increases serotonin, but also distracts from rumination, which will be addressed in Chapter 10.

Here is a small list of stimulating activities, with space underneath so you can add your own suggestions. Which list do you engage with the most? The least? What can you do to change this, so that you are receiving stimulation in all four zones? And how much stimulation do you need to thrive?

Physical	*Intellectual*	*Sensory*	*Social*
Exercise	Renovating	Craft	Hiking in a group
Hiking	Religious Services	Singing	Parties
Renovating	Debates	Bird watching	Discussion groups
Gardening	Playing a musical instrument	Being outdoors in all weather	Visiting friends/family
Fixing an engine	Reading inspiring books	Listening to music	Religious services
Yoga	Studying	Pleasant aromas	Volunteer work
Vigorous Massage	Learning a new skill	Eating spicy food	Singing in a choir
Swimming	Discussion groups	Cooking	Sports groups
Walking	Podcasts	Massage chairs	Your workplace

Winding Down

At night, by contrast, avoid stimulation, but continue to distract any unconstructive thoughts with winding down activities.

Two hours before bedtime, reduce all lighting in the house. Even better, live like the olden days: turn off all lights and light a candle instead. Engage in relaxing activities, like reading, tinkering, knitting. If you must work on the laptop or computer, dim the screen as low as possible (more on this in the following chapters). Avoid reading exciting books, watching TV or googling stimulating internet sites. TV programs and adverts are especially designed and timed to stimulate, so that you wake up and take notice. One of the techniques film producers use to increase suspense and excitement is to sequence a series of rapid scene changes. With each scene change, the light flashes from the screen and stimulates the viewer. Avoid TV before bed.

Activities that can help you wind down (add your own)

- Jigsaw puzzles
- Massage
- Gentle yoga or stretching
- Meditation
- Crochet
- Deep, slow breathing
- Tai Chi
- Crosswords and puzzles
- Prayer
- Relaxation music (see Reset Ten)
- A warm bath (but not too hot)
- A relaxing book
- Make a list of 100 things that make you feel good
- Relax on your porch or patio, enjoy the night and people watch

PRACTICAL APPLICATION

Day

- No matter how you feel, no matter what your mood, no matter where your thoughts — even if you're a walking nimbus cloud! — take charge of your daylight hours, and choose stimulating activities that will keep you active and moving all day, *even when you don't feel like it.*
- Choose at least one activity from each of the Physical, Intellectual, Sensory and Social pastimes each day.

- During the day, avoid any activity that involves closing the eyes or being in the dark for more than 10 minutes. If you use the meditation apps, do the exercises without closing your eyes.

Night

- Designing your new lifestyle routine can be one of your relaxation activities. Go over the list every night.
- Complete your daily Mood Log (Chapter 14).
- Studies have also shown that spending five minutes writing a comprehensive to-do list last thing at night results in overall improved sleep quality.[12]
- Add at least one activity to your Circadian Circle (page 16) that best fits with your daily commitments.

Once you have set up your new meal and activity patterns, and have adjusted house and device lighting, it is time to tackle a tougher issue: *sleep patterns*.

RESET 7: SLEEP SPOT-ON

*Keep your internal clock set
with a consistent sleep schedule.*

THE SCIENCE BEHIND IT

A typical night's sleep consists of four or five REM (when we dream) and non-REM cycles with occasional brief episodes of wakefulness. Most Stage 4 sleep occurs during the first two to three hours of sleep. As morning approaches, REM sleep occupies an increasing share of the sleep periods

Here is a diagram of an average healthy sleep pattern that demonstrates the variety of stages our brains and bodies go through overnight.

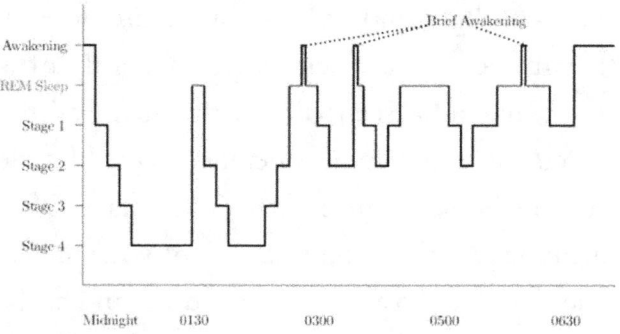

Those episodes of wakefulness can be distressing to people with depression or anxiety. But even the heaviest sleeper goes through a variety of stages through the night, and you can take comfort in this: sleep studies have shown that when people in overnight sleep labs report being awake for 'hours' during the night, their brain waves, recorded on the EEG, proved they were actually asleep.[13]

Sleep Disorders

There are three main variations of insomnia: waking too early, waking during the night, and Delayed Sleep Phase Disorder. Some forms of depression include *hypersomnia*, which is excessive sleepiness and trouble staying awake during the day. While a combination of these disorders is common, the point to note is that all abnormal sleep patterns have one thing in common: they mess with the brain chemistry and, if you are one of the sensitive folk, can trigger mood disorders.

If you find it difficult to fall asleep before midnight and then have difficulty waking up in the morning, you probably have some form of Delayed Sleep Phase Disorder. As with all nonorganic — that is: not medically or mechanically caused — sleep disorders, this condition is probably related to a *sensitivity* to light and dark, temperature, food and other factors that influence sleep, either permanently or at certain phases of life, like adolescence.[14] Treatment for all nonorganic sleep disorders involves careful adherence to the lifestyle changes outlined in this book. It means that if you have DSPD, along with your mood disorder, you must adapt your life around the hours of the clock, set up a consistent routine and find enjoyable daytime activities. While nightclubs make a healthy profit from fit young adults who can dance, drink and party to rave music and strobe lights until 2am, be in bed and asleep 2.30am, and fully functional at work by 7am, this lifestyle is definitely out for anyone prone to mood disorders.

However, if you do miss the nightclub scene, there is a fantastic alternative: *morning rave parties* in most major cities, like www.daybreaker.com and morninggloryville.com that usually start around 6am. While not everyone's cup-of-tea, these alcohol-free dance parties, that also offer 'free hugs,' are ideal for setting the biological clock and combatting depression: bright lights, loud music and vigorous dancing *first thing in the morning.*

Melatonin Medication?

Little is known about the long-term effects of taking melatonin medication as a sleep aid for people with depression, and studies have even shown that it can even worsen depression.[15] Furthermore, you can save your money, because all you need are a few hours of dim lighting or darkness and your brain naturally produces it free of charge!

Just Right

The average adult needs six to eight hours of sleep per night. Staying in bed in the dark any longer than eight hours will contribute to poor sleep the following night. So it is vital to set your alarm for no more than 8–9 hours from the time you lie down to go to sleep. Therefore, if you hit the sack at 10pm, set the alarm for 6am.

The biggest challenge of this program will be this: *getting out of bed with the alarm and into the light of day, despite your low mood.* But if you lie around in bed after that time, you'll delay the much-needed serotonin onset, delay the melatonin production 12–14 hours later, and your mood will stay low. And that is why people with depression often feel worse first thing in the morning: their brain chemistry is still registering night-time, and their day-time chemistry is delayed. The way to shift this is to get vertical, start moving, and get out into the light. If you can conquer this biggest obstacle, you are already on your road to renewal. Get up and treat yourself as someone worthy of love and care everyday, whether you feel like it or not.

Catch the Night Wave

Approximately two hours after being in the dark, and fasting, we begin to feel sleepy. For poor sleepers, it is important to catch that first wave before it subsides. Each cycle lasts approximately 90 minutes, so if you miss one wave, it might be another 90 minutes until your next sleep wave.

Hypersomnia

Sleeping too much also causes imbalances in our brain chemistry, and assuming you've been thoroughly checked for underlying medical causes, then exactly the same guidelines in this book apply.

PRACTICAL APPLICATION

Create a cool, dark and quiet sleep sanctuary

- Begin your wind-down bedtime routine at least half an hour before you go to bed. This includes brushing teeth, shower, wash etc.
- Reserve your bedroom for sleep and other restful activities, like reading and meditation, and for no more than 8–9 hours at night only. Don't work, nap or rest in your bedroom during the day.
- Banish the television, computer, and phone from your bedroom.
- Your bedside light should have the lowest possible lux measurement, and a red bulb if possible.
- Room temperature should be between 60F (15C) and 67F (20C) and humidity: 30–60% for optimal sleep conditions. You can buy room temperature and humidity monitors for under $10. Humidifers can be bought from pharmacies or department stores.
- Keep your bed on the cool side, with 100% cotton sheets, and light blankets only.
- Use a comfortable mattress that has robust back-support. A sagging mattress will leave you tired and aching.

Routine

- Set your alarm to wake you eight hours from when you switch out the light to go to sleep. It is essential that you don't sleep any longer than eight hours. If you want to control your mood fluctuations, don't sleep in: ever. Even on weekends. Getting out of bed when the alarm goes off is essential.

- 🖥 The iPhone has an inbuilt easy-to-use App called Bedtime that is ideal for guiding your routine. It will alert you when it's time to get ready for bed, and wake you eight hours after your nominated sleep time.
  » Tap on the Clock
  » Tap on the On button for Bedtime
  » Tap Options
  » Tap all seven days
  » Tap Bedtime Reminder and choose 30–45 minutes
  » Choose your Wake Up Sound
- Even if you don't sleep well, or enough, get up anyway after 8–9 hours and carry on as if you had slept. Just go about your day normally, no matter how bad you feel. Your biological clock is being set by these actions, and fatigue will disappear if you persist.
- Get fully dressed down to your shoes: no slippers and dressing gowns, or sloppy clothes.
- Make your bed: it all helps!
- Choose your 2–3 hour wind down time and your 8-hour sleeping timeslot, and add these your Circadian Circle (page 16).

Surviving the night

- If you wake during the night, remember this: you are just switching sleep stages, and your brain is probably asleep, even though you *think* you're wide awake.
- Avoid watching the clock or checking the time if you wake.

- If distressing thoughts are overwhelming, read a relaxing book in the dimmest light possible, or play a game on a dimmed and blue-light filtered phone for a while. But stay in as much dark as possible until the morning.
- It is very unpleasant to lie awake with distressing thoughts, but persistence and endurance are key to re-programming your sleeping patterns.

Waking Too Early

- If you have slept fewer than seven hours, stay in bed in the dark until eight hours have elapsed, then get up and into the light. Early waking will pass if you develop a 24 hour routine.

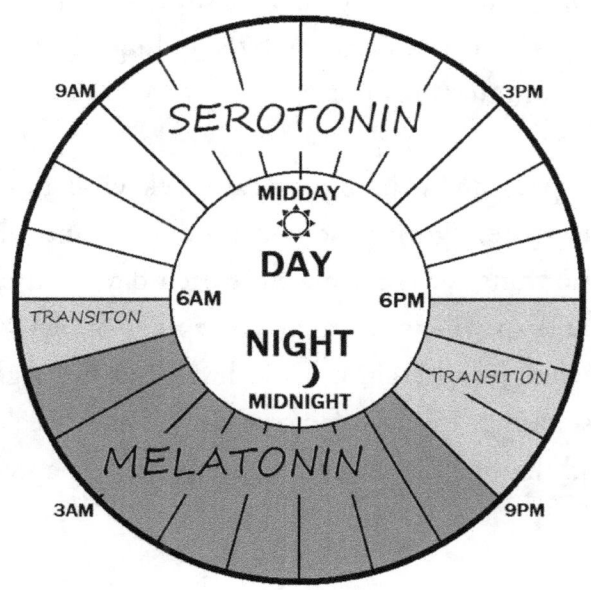

💻 FREE APPS FOR SLEEPING, WAKING, TRACKING AND RELAXATION

- www.sleepcycle.com Sleep Cycle tracks and analyzes your sleep patterns with the use of the phone's microphone. It gently wakes you at the optimal time.
- www.runtastic.com/en/apps/sleepbetter Sleep Better also tracks your sleep and offer tips.
- Sleepdays and Pillow: are iPhone apps with trackers and analyzers.
- www.calm.com Award winning app for relaxation.
- www.lightawake.biz this app can be set to wake you with a flashing blue light.
- www.spinmealarm.com ($) An alarm clock where the only way to turn off the ringer is by standing up in a vertical position and turning around.

When you program your biological clock with information from food intake, lighting, activity, and a routine where you do the same things at the same time each day, your sleep will improve, and so will your mood. Sleeping 'Spot-On' means neither sleeping too much, nor too little, but just right. Temperature is another external factor that you can tweak to your benefit, and that will be the subject of the next chapter.

RESET 8: TWEAK YOUR CORE BODY TEMPERATURE

Keep your internal clock set with the right temperature at the right time.

THE SCIENCE BEHIND IT

Temperature also affects sleep quality and productivity during the day, plus it feeds information into our body-clocks. The principle here is: *warm during the day, and cool at night.* Warmth (but not too warm) increases serotonin, and cool depletes it.

Body temperature normally fluctuates over the day following our biological clock, with the lowest levels around 4am and the highest in the late afternoon, around 4–6pm. Note also the dip just after lunch when some cultures have traditionally taken afternoon naps.

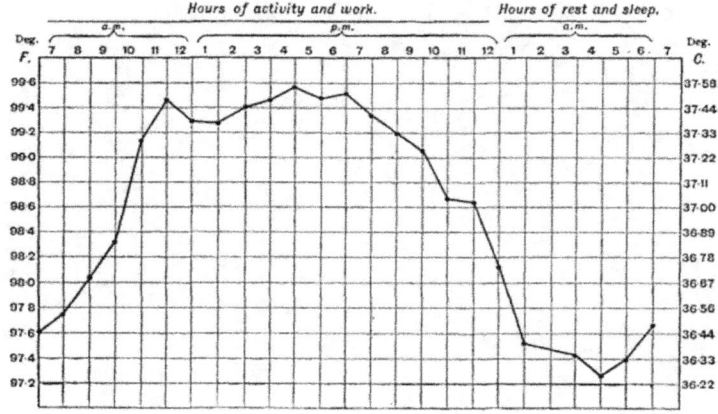

External factors that increase our core body temperature include exercise, food, warm clothing and emotions, whereas fasting and rest decreases it. While the tweaks described in this book will address such external factors, medications, medical conditions and certain life phases, like menopause, can also affect core temperature and need to be treated by the doctor first. It is also important to note that alcohol decreases our day temperature while increasing it at the night, and we want the reverse to happen. So alcohol will confuse our brain chemistry and potentially cause sleep deficits. Avoid alcohol if you have a mood disorder.[16]

Productivity — a reliable measuring stick for mood — increases or decreases according to workplace temperatures. Studies on work output show that raising the temperature from 67F (20C) to 75F (25C) in an office greatly increases productivity.[17]

PRACTICAL APPLICATION

- Temperatures between 60F (15C) and 67F (20C) are optimal for sleeping, and temperatures above 75F (24C) and below 54F (12C) are disruptive to sleep.[18]
- During your waking hours, the ideal temperature is 77F (25C), so keep a temperature gauge in your home and workplace and adjust the heating and cooling accordingly.
- If your workplace is cold, take a portable heater and wear thermals. Even if you can change the thermostat in your office, chances are that the warmth doesn't get evenly distributed across the room.

Another factor that has been shown to have some influence on mood and productivity is sound, and its beneficial uses will be outlined in the next chapter.

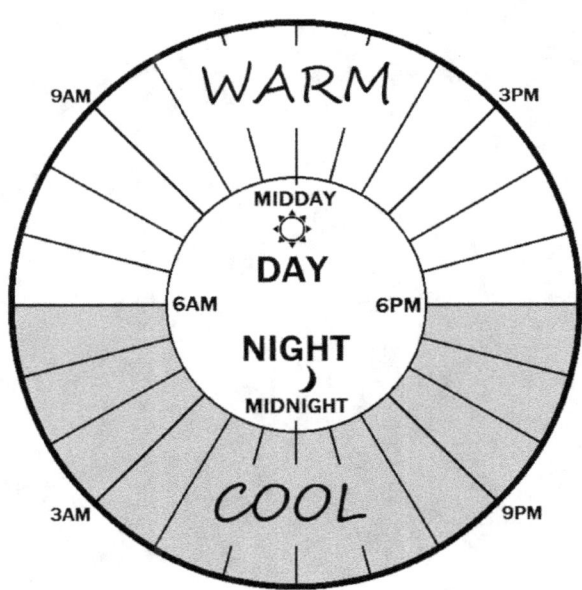

RESET 9: FINE-TUNE YOUR ENVIRONMENT TO LOWER ANXIETY

How ambient sound can allay anxiety and increase energy.

THE SCIENCE BEHIND IT

While your bedroom should be a cool, dark and quiet retreat, your day areas should be warm, light, and not *too* quiet.

"Pin Drop Syndrome"

Sound waves aren't a therapy, but a tweak to the environment that may or may not work for you. Studies have shown that too quiet workplaces decrease productivity and increase anxiety. While people generally differ, super-quiet environments can make some feel lonelier. Some workplaces are now introducing 'noise machines' with chitchat and occasional laughter, and productivity has increased. The optimal level of background noise should be between 20–60 decibels. Most humans cannot hear under 20db, and 60db is about the level of a quiet conversation.[19]

Noise Pitch

Like light waves, sound waves also vary in frequency. Music with a higher pitch and faster beat will be more stimulating, and useful for the day. Low pitched sound-waves are slow, and therefore more relaxing. Gregorian chanting and Tibetan 'throat music' is usually gentle, low in pitch, and very relaxing.

PRACTICAL APPLICATION

The following ideas will add pleasant background sounds to your day:
- https://mynoise.net is a site created by sound engineer Stephane Pigeon, which is filled with dozens of high-quality, customizable nature recordings, relaxing soundscapes and atmospheric effects.
- A fish tank
- An indoor water fountain
- Wind chimes
- Music
- And open door or window

At night:
- Keep sounds low and slow in the evening.
- Wear ear earplugs if there is noise outside of your bedroom that you cannot control.

Now that we have addressed the external factors, we will target unhelpful habits.

RESET 10: HALT THE RUMINATION

"Do not distress yourself with dark imaginings. Many fears are born of fatigue and loneliness."
(a line from *Desiderata*)

When Max Ehrmann penned Desiderata in 1927, there was limited knowledge about the effects of neuro-chemistry on mood and thought content. Still, a US psychiatrist saw the value in the poem's counsel and sought permission to distribute copies to soldiers during WWII, and in 1970 it was turned into a hit song. Ehrmann's words went viral because they expressed universal wisdom, and a now proven scientific fact: *euthymic brains work better.*

THE SCIENCE BEHIND IT

Every now and again intense thinking can liberate us because it can foster awareness and positive change, but 'dark imaginings' can also become a fruitless habit. Ruminating is the act of repetitively mulling over a thought or a problem without completion, and the themes typically orbit around personal inadequacy and worthlessness. The irony is, that, instead of moving forward, the rumination itself stunts creativity and genuine insight by capturing precious brain resources, and distracting us from the actual solution.[20][21]

Although the lifestyle changes outlined in this book will improve mood and thought content, Cognitive Behavior Therapy (CBT) that is specifically targeted at rumination can be helpful. A recently developed variant of CBT designed to directly target rumination (Rumination-focused CBT) involves switching the focus from unhelpful rumination to helpful forms.[22]

PRACTICAL INTERVENTION

- Work with a Cognitive Behavior Therapist where possible. If not, you can find CBT workbooks that target depression and rumination. Two self-help books that have been researched and found effective are: *Feeling Good: The New Mood Therapy* by David Burns, and *Control Your Depression, Revised Edition*, by Peter Lewinsohn.[23]
- Bring your awareness to ruminating and note that it isn't helpful. Remind yourself that depression distorts the truth, and that these fears are born of fatigue from a depressed mind, not reality.
- Track back. Ask yourself: what triggered this return to rumination? Write down the trigger and the thoughts that preceded and followed it.
- Find something funny about your situation: humor can help.
- Think "Stop!" or even say it out loud and break the loop.
- Visualize taking your current thoughts and putting them in the bin.
- Another technique is to exaggerate your ruminations: indulge in 30 minutes of purposeful, mindful rumination. Then keep busy for the rest of the day with your exercise program, work and normal activities, and once your brain chemistry is healthy again, the ruminations will naturally subside.

🖥 BEST FREE INTERACTIVE CBT APPS

- Pacifica www.thinkpacifica.com has a range of easy to use tools, like a mood diary, quick meditations to address destructive thoughts, goal setting, healthy habit and exercise reminders and more.
- www.stopbreathethink.com asks you to 'check in' physically, mentally and emotionally, then offers recommended meditations and resources adapted to your input.
- www.happify.com has a similar set up with questions about your life and thoughts, and a program is created for you based on that.
- http://sam-app.org.uk Sam targets anxiety and ruminations.

Keep Busy

- Tidy the house
- Water the garden or do some weeding
- Fix the car
- Listen to the radio or your iPod
- Take out the bins
- Go grocery shopping
- Declutter one room
- Bake something
- Sort out your closet
- Join and engage with uplifting Facebook groups

If you have been following the whole program, your day should by now be full of healthy activities, even if you still don't feel fully functional. There is another habit that needs to be addressed: drug and alcohol misuse.

RESET 11: AVOID THE SELF MEDICATING TRAP

Avoid drugs or alcohol.

THE SCIENCE BEHIND IT

'Self-medicating' is a term used by mental health professionals to describe a patient's desperate attempts to conquer his body's lack of obedience through substances. Unfortunately, people with mood disorders tend towards higher incidence of illicit drug use, and misuse of prescription drugs or alcohol, because they are attempting to *self-medicate*. But this *whipping* the body-clock into submission with substances is about as useful as thumping a laptop that doesn't work: it might feel good in the moment, but only aggravates the condition in the long term. Instead, our body, and therefore brain, needs to be fed *messages* with food, light, dark, and other such stimuli, and at specific times.

As we read in the chapter on sleep, each sleep-cycle takes roughly 90 minutes, and to feel rested we need four or five of these brain-wave sequences per night. But drugs and alcohol can interfere with these natural cycles. So, while these substances might help us fall sleep in the first place, our ANS doesn't know what's going on. Disturbed sleep causes imbalances in our Circadian Rhythms, and further contributes to mood disorders.

PRACTICAL APPLICATION

- The bottom line: avoid all illicit drugs.
- Of prescription drugs, only take the prescribed dosage.
- Avoid alcohol: alcohol is a depressant and it interferes with core body temperatures that in turn regulate your sleep-wake cycle. So if you must have a glass of beer or wine, limit it to one, consumed with a meal, and well before your fasting window.

12: RESET FOR TEENAGERS

THE SCIENCE BEHIND IT

Depending on the source, the percentage of teens suffering mood disorders is somewhere between 5–20%. Furthermore, anti-depressant medication is often ineffective, and can be even harmful for this age group.[24]

It is also widely reported that teens tend to have Delayed Sleep Phases, and there are some data that suggest adolescents go through at least one phase of circadian cycle sensitivity during their growth years. See Reset 7 for more details on DSPD.

Teenage Sleep Patterns

Teenagers need 8-10 hours of sleep, and it is often disrupted due to social events, heavy homework loads, food at all hours, and late-night screen use. Many parents allow their teens to sleep in on weekends, believing this to be beneficial. But sleeping in is often counterproductive and, while teens, and even their parents, may feel like they are doing their bodies a favor by sleeping in, they actually aren't. Sleeping late on Saturday and Sunday may fill that deficit, but it creates a bigger problem in the end. It allows your teen's biological clock to drift further away from the external clock. The result is that the body-clock is thrown out of whack, which makes it much more difficult to get to sleep the next night, and then wake up at a required hour the following day. Wide awake in the middle of the night, yet with everyone else in bed, the teen resorts to screens or food which, as we have seen, make the problem worse.

It's essential to train teens in good sleep hygiene habits. Tell your teen that you are '*melatoninizing* the house' when you switch off all the non-essential lights, store screens away, pull the blinds and curtains, and begin to wind down. Twelve hours later, you can *serotoninize* by opening the curtains, being active and eating well. The words melatoninize and serotoninize are, of course, invented, and may be useful for boosting your teen's understanding of their body chemistry, and the environment's affects on it.

SCHEDULING

Is an idle mind the devil's playground?

Until the last few decades, British boarding school regimes guaranteed their teenage pupils had no free time at all. Every waking moment was chockfull in activities: from daily chapel, lessons, formal dining, sport, debate, army cadets, evening lectures and prep — six days per week. Even Sundays afforded no idle time, with two church services and supervised letter writing.

But during the 1970s, an aversion to 'over-scheduling' became popular and it was claimed that too many extra-curricular activities was damaging to children, that 'boredom' was beneficial, and 'down time' essential. But recent data show just the contrary: active teens, engaged in extra curricular activities after school and on weekends, have greater overall wellbeing, and are less likely to engage in risky activities, like drugs, alcohol and sex, which can cause or exacerbate mood disorders.

Furthermore, the brain's prefrontal cortex, responsible for organization and impulse control, is still developing until the early 20s. But rather than expanding, as it does in the first few years of life, the teen brain is undergoing a stage of 'synaptic pruning,' which means the excess synapses — the unused connections between the nerve endings — are being trimmed away. According to neuroscientists, whatever your teen is spending most time on, those synapses will stay, while the others will be pruned. So quality activities are vital to a teen's well being and development.[25]

Many teens incline towards bad habits when left to themselves, and since their prefrontal cortex is still developing, 'down time' usually means 'screen time,' and we can't expect them to have the same organizational skills as adults. So teens — especially teens with depression — need direction, guidance with their 'free time,' and assistance with organization. While down-time might work well for mature adults, too much freedom could be detrimental for many teens.[26]

PRACTICAL APPLICATION

Teenagers with mood disorders will need extra parental guidance, encouragement and role modelling to follow the suggestions in this book.

- Engage your teen in a thoroughly scientific discussion, reviewing the biological clock, brain chemistry, and the Autonomic Nervous System, and how these are programmed by what we do. Externalizing the problem as a scientific matter promotes insight, and the quest for a solution seems less threatening and more empowering.
- Prioritize good habits and, with their cooperation, set up a routine based on all the suggestions in this book. Create a written plan together using the Circadian Circle on page 16.
- While you don't have to exactly return to the era of British boarding school regimes, keep your teen occupied with a wide variety of quality extra curricular activities, household chores, a part time job, family meals and events, outings etc.
- With a teen who has been used to staying up late on a screen and sleeping in, begin morning light therapy which, depending on where you live, can be either a light-box or opened curtains and blinds. Start on a Saturday, and at around 9am, a few hours after the body temperature has started to rise. The timing can be moved earlier by 30 minutes every 2–3 days or an hour per week, until the desired wake time is achieved.

- Once established, maintain the same wake-up time on weekends, as during the week. Open their curtains and blinds at the same agreed-upon time every morning, and expose them to sunlight. Allow no more than an extra half hour of sleep-in on weekends.
- Parents should role model the same healthy and structured routine they want for your teens.
- Keep to a strict 'lights-out' bedtime for the whole family at the same time every night.
- Parents should keep all electronics and phones stored or locked away from late night temptation. Give your teen half an hour notice before the specified device switch-off time, so they can finish what they are doing.
- Ban TV or computer gaming habits during the day. You want your teen to be up and active during daylight hours.
- Avoid bright lights three hours before bedtime. Switch off as many lights as possible, except for lamps with orange or red bulbs. Change their room light bulbs to red.
- Add Nightshift and f.lux Apps to their gadgets (see page 40).

The Value of Pets

If you don't have one already, consider getting a dog. Not only will it provide something else to focus on, but your teen will have to walk the dog every morning and evening, which encourages them to exercise and be outdoors.

13 REGENERATE: CREATE YOUR PERSONALIZED PLAN

*"Think in the morning. Act in the noon.
Eat in the evening. Sleep in the night."*
(William Blake)

If you have been filling in the Circadian Circle as you read, you will by now have a visual picture of your new lifestyle. If a list works better for you, here is a sample. Create a personalized plan to fit your lifestyle, climate, season and daily commitments.

Consistency is key: keep your meals, sleep and wake times the same every day, seven days a week.

6am: wake up.
6–6:30am: *if still dark* SAD Light therapy for 30 mins.
Hot shower.
7am: breakfast.
7.30am: walk or exercise in daylight.
8:30–midday: Work or continuous activities in 77F (25C) temperatures, preferably outdoors or in as much light as possible.
12–1pm: Lunch.
4pm: Last coffee, tea, soft drinks or chocolate for the day.
6pm: Dinner and finish all eating before 7pm. Water only from then on until 7am the following day.
7pm: If it is not dark yet, draw blinds and curtains. Make the house as dark as possible. Switch off blue-emitting lights, like LEDs and fluorescent lights. Activate the blue filters on your screens, if they are not automatically programmed, or wear blue-blocking glasses.
Engage in your chosen relaxation activities.

9:30pm: begin your bed time routine. Sit in bed, fill in your mood-log and write out a list of what you have to do tomorrow. Do some slow gentle breathing meditation.
10pm: check alarm is set, then lights out.

SAMPLE SHOPPING LIST

- Two temperature gauges: for bedroom and day areas.
- Blue light blocking glasses.
- SAD lamp.
- Very low wattage lamp for bedside table with a red bulb.
- A bright 5500–6000K light bulb with a high lumen count for your day areas.

14 REVISE: YOUR DAILY MOOD LOG

Daily Mood Log

Time / Day	1	2	3	4	5	6	7	8	9	10	11	12	13	14	15	16	17	18	19	20	21	22	23	24	What helped/hindered?
1																									
2																									
3																									
4																									
5																									
6																									
7																									
8																									
9																									
10																									
11																									
12																									
13																									
14																									
15																									
16																									
17																									
18																									
19																									
20																									
21																									
22																									
23																									
24																									
25																									
26																									
27																									
28																									
29																									
30																									
31																									

Remember that the goal of this program described in the introduction was euthymia, which means a stable, non-depressed mental state or mood. Unlike *happiness*, which tends to change with life's ups and downs, euthymia is not an emotion. When you are euthymic, you are in control of your thoughts, mood and actions, you get your life back, your sleep improves, the daily routine doesn't seem like a chore anymore, you quit wondering when you're going to feel better, and you suddenly find yourself being creative and productive again.

PRODUCTIVITY DEFINED

What do we mean by productivity? Being productive doesn't mean composing the next musical masterpiece or designing an award winning computer program, but just completing simple tasks: emptying a bin, buying some milk, paying a bill, or pulling out a weed in the garden. These small steps pave the way for more steps and create a feeling of self-mastery.

One of these small steps is to begin your daily mood log as soon as possible, so that you can track your progress.
- Fill in yesterday and today using red and blue pencils if possible.
- Rate your 'blue' mood in blue pen, -1 a little low, -2 moderately low, -3 severely low.

- Rate your 'red' mood in red pen, <u>0</u> unsure/in between, <u>+1</u> euthymic, <u>+2</u> euthymic and productive <u>+3</u> euthymic and fully functional.
- Black out the boxes of the hours you are sleeping, and put a line through the ones where you are lying in bed but awake.

    ■ = sleeping ◻ = lying in bed
- In the comments box, note down anything that helped or hindered, and review it nightly.
- The best time to fill in your log is last thing at night.

15 REMISSION MASTERY

Once you have reset your body-clock and your depression symptoms have gone into remission, it is essential that you stick to your new lifestyle changes, even if you feel great. Although a night out or a late meal every so often shouldn't cause a relapse, you will have more energy to return to base and keep to your routine when you are well. But caution is needed as everyone is different, and some people *can* relapse after just one or two sleep disturbances. The main point is that remission is not a time to return to poor lifestyle patterns and self neglect, but the ideal time to solidify your new habits and goals, and continue to do the same things at the same time every day.

If you have followed all the advice in this book for two to three weeks you should be well on the way to recovery. However, if you are still depressed, see your doctor. You may have an underlying disorder that needs addressing, or psychological issues that need further investigations. But don't give up on the strategies in *Depression Reset*: they *will* help along with your other interventions.

I wish you all the best for a bright future and leave you with this perennial piece of wisdom: *Desiderata*, which is Latin for '*Desired Things.*'

Go placidly amid the noise and the haste and remember what peace there may be in silence. As far as possible, without surrender, be on good terms with all persons. Speak your truth quietly and clearly; and listen to others, even to the dull and the ignorant; they too have their story. Avoid loud and aggressive persons; they are vexatious to the spirit. If you compare yourself with others, you may become vain or bitter, for always there will be greater and lesser persons than yourself. Enjoy your achievements as well as your plans. Keep interested in your own career, however humble; it is a real possession in the changing fortunes of time. Exercise caution in your business affairs, for the world is full of trickery. But let this not blind you to what virtue there is; many persons strive for high ideals, and everywhere life is full of heroism. Be yourself. Especially, do not feign affection. Neither be cynical about love; for in the face of all aridity and disenchantment it is as perennial as the grass. Take kindly the counsel of the years, gracefully surrendering the things of youth.

Nurture strength of spirit to shield you in sudden misfortune. But do not distress yourself with dark imaginings. Many fears are born of fatigue and loneliness. Beyond a wholesome discipline, be gentle with yourself. You are a child of the universe no less than the trees and the stars; you have a right to be here. And whether or not it is clear to you, no doubt the universe is unfolding as it should. Therefore, be at peace with God, whatever you conceive Him to be. And whatever your labors and aspirations, in the noisy confusion of life, keep peace in your soul. With all its sham, drudgery and broken dreams, it is still a beautiful world. Be cheerful. Strive to be happy.

"Desiderata" by Max Ehrmann

APPENDIX 1: SLEEP APNEA

Which famous British prime minister had strange sleep habits, was overweight, smoked cigars, and famously described his fluctuating mood as The Black Dog?

Yes, Winston Churchill, and he had all the classic signs of someone who was suffering from Sleep Apnea, though there were no EEGs to test for it then, and no CPAP machines to treat it.

Sleep apnea is a sleep disorder characterized by pauses in breathing or periods of shallow breathing during sleep ('apnea' means 'without breathing'). Each pause can last for a few seconds to a few minutes and they happen many times a night, playing havoc with even the soundest sleep cycles. In the most common form, this 'pause' follows loud snoring. Only recently have professionals begun looking at the links between Sleep Apnea, mood disorders or other mental illness. Because of the disruption of sleep, and the fatigue during the day, brain chemistry becomes confused and can lead to long term mood disorders until treated. And because psychotropic and anti-depressant medications can cause significant weight gain, which can cause Sleep Apnea, which causes insomnia, which causes serotonin and melatonin imbalances, which can cause depression or other mental illness relapses, it is vital to be thoroughly screened for it.

There are three forms of sleep apnea:
- The most common form is Obstructive (OSA), the most common cause being obesity. Also enlarged tonsils, a small airway and smoking can cause OSA. In Winston Churchill's photos, he shows the classic signs of someone prone to OSA: fat around the neck, and smoking.
- Central (CSA) is neurological.
- Both OSA and CSA together

It is essential to be checked for this if you have depression, because it is very treatable.

APPENDIX 2: NIGHT SHIFT

As a nurse I have worked many nightshifts. Follow the guidelines in this book, eating during your nightshift, fasting from two hours before going to sleep, and maintaining the fast for at least 12 hours during, and either side of, your sleeping hours. A dark bedroom and black-out blinds are essential.

But if you are prone to depression and also do shiftwork you may need to consider changing your job altogether. Prioritize your mental health, even if that means a career change with a lower salary.

APPENDIX 3: JET LAG

Jet Lag is caused by switching to a different time-zone, and researchers say it takes a healthy adult around four days to change the clock around, and meal timing is key.

If you are flying from London to New York, you would begin fasting during the night hours that correspond with New York, even if it's the middle of the day in London. You would eat breakfast at, say 4pm, as that would correspond to that time in New York. For best results, fasting should begin 16 hours from your last meal in London until breakfast in New York.

If you travel across time-zones, yet are prone to depression, it is essential to plan for the change in your biological clock a few days before by following the guidelines in this book.

🖥 www.jetlagrooster.com

1   American Psychiatric Association, *DSM-5*, 2013

2   https://www.asx.com.au/asxpdf/20131216/pdf/42lmy913xxyp9s.pdf

3   *Your Brain On Chocolate* (2017) https://www.health.harvard.edu/blog/your-brain-on-chocolate-2017081612179

4   *A randomised controlled trial of dietary improvement for adults with major depression* (2017) https://bmcmedicine.biomedcentral.com/articles/10.1186/s12916-017-0791-y

5   U.S. Environmental Protection Agency. 1989. *Report to Congress on indoor air quality*: Volume 2. EPA/400/1-89/001C. Washington, DC.

6   Linking Light Exposure and Subsequent Sleep: A Field Polysomnography Study in Humans. https://www.ncbi.nlm.nih.gov/pubmed/29040758

7   Blue light has a dark side (2017) https://www.health.harvard.edu/staying-healthy/blue-light-has-a-dark-side

8   Action spectrum for melatonin regulation in humans: evidence for a novel circadian photoreceptor. https://www.ncbi.nlm.nih.gov/pubmed/11487664?dopt=Abstract

8   *Blue light: A blessing or a curse?* Science Direct, 2015, Cristina Caramelo Gomes, Sandra Preto

9   *Effects of blue light on the circadian system and eye physiology* (2016) https://www.ncbi.nlm.nih.gov/pmc/articles/PMC4734149/

10 *The Benefits of Exercise for the Clinically Depressed* (2004) https://www.ncbi.nlm.nih.gov/pmc/articles/PMC474733/

11 *Long-Term Adherence to Health Behavior Change* (2013) https://www.ncbi.nlm.nih.gov/pmc/articles/PMC4988401/

12 The British Psychological Society (2018) https://digest.bps.org.uk/2018/01/15/researchers-say-this-5-minute-technique-could-help-you-fall-asleep-more-quickly/

13 Michael H. Bonnet and Sarah E. Moore V.A. Hospital and Department of Psychology, University of Cincinnati, Cincinnati, Ohio, U.S.A, 1982, *The Threshold of Sleep: Perception of Sleep as a Function of Time Asleep and Auditory Threshold*

14 *Therapeutics for Circadian Rhythm Sleep Disorders* (2010) https://www.ncbi.nlm.nih.gov/pmc/articles/PMC3020104/pdf/nihms-229698.pdf

15 Carman JS, Post RM, Buswell R, Goodwin FK, 'Negative effects of melatonin on depression.' *American Journal of Psychiatry* 1976 133.

16 Danel T, Libersa C, Touitou Y. The effect of alcohol consumption on the circadian control of human core body temperature is time dependent. Am J Physiol Regul Integr Comp Physiol 2001;281:R52-R55

17 *Linking Environmental Linking Environmental Conditions to Productivity Conditions to Productivity* (2004) http://ergo.human.cornell.edu/Conferences/EECE_IEQ%20and%20Productivity_ABBR.pdf

18 Onen SH, Onen F, Bailly D, Parquet P. Prevention *and treatment of sleep disorders through regulation of sleeping habits.* Presse Med.1994; Mar 12; 23(10): 485-9

19 *BBC cheers up lonely staff with the chit-chat machine* (1999) https://www.theguardian.com/media/1999/oct/14/bbc.uknews

20 *Rumination and Impaired Resource Allocation in Depression* (2009) https://web.stanford.edu/group/mood/docs120610/Levens_Muhtadie_Gotlib_2009.pdf

21 *More than sad: Depression affects your ability to think* (2016) https://www.health.harvard.edu/blog/sad-depression-affects-ability-think-201605069551

22 Depressive Rumination and Co-Morbidity: Evidence for Brooding as a Transdiagnostic Process (2009) https://www.ncbi.nlm.nih.gov/pmc/articles/PMC2731158/pdf/10942_2009_Article_98.pdf

23 *A Guide To What Works For Depression,* Jorm, Allen, Morgan, Ryan, Purcell, beyondblue.org.au

24 *Comparative efficacy and tolerability of antidepressants for major depressive disorder in children and adolescents* (2016) http://www.thelancet.com/journals/lancet/article/PIIS0140-6736(16)30385-3/abstract

25 *Adolescent Brains are Works in Progress* (2000) https://www.pbs.org/wgbh/pages/frontline/shows/teenbrain/work/adolescent.html

26 *The Over-Scheduling Myth* (2008)

www.ingramcontent.com/pod-product-compliance
Lightning Source LLC
Chambersburg PA
CBHW072054290426
44110CB00014B/1678